# Seeking God?

Floyd E. Schneider

# Keybobby
## Books

For more information about Keybobby Books,
visit our websites:

www.floydschneider.com and
www.cristineschneiderblog.com

ISBN-13:978-0-9630214-1-0

# DEDICATION

To all my students
who tolerate(d) my challenging questions.
A special thanks to Jordan Fischer, Jeff Glessner, Travis
Hantz, and Chelsea Sundblad for help with editing. ☺

# CONTENTS

# CHAPTER ONE

---

## TURN THE PAGE

If you are not interested in God, then you are reading the wrong book.

What is God like? Does it matter what God is like? No one will read a book about God unless that person is interested in God. Therefore we need to establish the importance of God first. From God's perspective He is important. From within the human heart, however, God's importance depends on a person's desire to answer life's most perplexing questions: Is there a God? What happens after death? Why is there evil in the world?

If a person has no interest in these questions, then that person will probably not have much interest in God, who is the only one who has the answers to these questions. This book assumes that those who have no interest in God will not even be reading this sentence. A person with a little interest might read a few pages because a friend gave him the book, or it was the only book on the table during a visit to the dentist, and reading a book about God might take the mind off the coming pain.

When most people begin to think about God, they start with themselves. Anthropologists tell us that a person's perception of God does not begin or develop in a vacuum, but is influenced by his culture, upbringing, position in life, and a dozen other items. However, anthropologists have not been able to discover the reason why some people are interested in God and others are not. Actually, a person's surroundings do *not* influence what he wants (Hear anthropologists boo-ing!). Two different people can come from identical backgrounds and live in identical environments, yet one chooses *to want* to know about God and the other *not to want* to know about God. Poor people seek God because they need Him, and poor people do not seek God because they assume He is evil for allowing them to be poor. Healthy people think that

God is important and thank Him for their good health, and healthy people have no time to think about God at all. Free people thank God for their freedom, and free people reject God because they don't believe they need Him. Slaves thank God that they are still alive, and slaves reject God because they are slaves. Politicians, doctors, fathers, and wives all choose to answer the question, "Why does it matter?" with a "yes" or a "no," regardless of their upbringing, social standing, culture, government, or climate. No *clear* answer[1] exists as to why some people want to know about God and others do not. They just do or do not. Theologians have argued for centuries about the ultimate reason for this situation, but no single theological system has been developed that provides a satisfactory answer for everyone. So we are left with the simple question, "Is discovering God important to *me*?" If not, please give this book to someone else to read. If yes, turn the page and keep reading.

---

[1] Apart from various theological systems that claim to have a clear answer, while vigorously disagreeing with other theological systems making the same claim with different answers.

# CHAPTER TWO

---

## PLURALISM

In order to learn about God, we need to identify the most appropriate sources that present us with the best information about Him. However, before looking for, and at, those sources, we need to answer two questions. The questions are different from each other, but they should be dealt with at the same time..

First question: Do all religions lead to God? This is called "pluralism." Is pluralism the correct way of looking at all religions? Second question: Should different religions be allowed to co-exist in the same society? How should we define and practice "tolerance" among religions?

I spent fifteen years[2] living in Austria. In the smaller towns and villages, religious tolerance was not one of that culture's strongest points. Roman Catholicism, as the majority religion, and Lutheranism in the minority, determined that all other religions were to be considered as cults. There was (and is), however, more religious freedom in Europe than in Muslim countries. The Muslims could build mosques and worship freely in Europe. Christians, conversely by any name, did not have those same freedoms in Muslim countries.

The great benefit of pluralistic spirituality *in a free country* is that it promotes tolerance between religions. If a person can believe in Buddha and someone else can believe in Allah and someone else in Jesus without anyone going to war with one another, then tolerance exists between those religions. Most wars have been caused by religions that believed they needed to cleanse the earth of "heretics," i.e., those who belonged to a different faith. During the Middle Ages the only real difference between official Christendom and Islam was the shape of the sword. Tolerance, therefore, in this contest of religions is good. People stay alive longer in a tolerant society.

---

[2] 1980-1995.

Pluralism, on the other hand, leads to intellectual suicide. To claim that all religions lead to the same end overlooks the actual beliefs of millions of adherents of all the diverse religions. The world's religious claims contradict one another in almost every area. They all have common forms, like prayer, but their beliefs refuse to agree with each other at the most basic levels.

Hinduism, for instance, believes in an array of gods ("polytheism"), with each god carrying out some function for those who choose to follow that god. Guru Nanak, however, a one-time Hindu, rejected this array of gods, and founded Sikhism, which believes in just one god (monotheism). Buddhism, on the other hand, sprang up from Siddhartha Gautama, who rejected Hinduism in favor of no gods. Technically, that leads to atheism, but Gautama was more of an agnostic, because he didn't really care if any gods existed at all. His followers eventually chose to worship Gautama. They are fortunate that he has not risen from the dead to condemn them for their misdirection of his religion.[3]

The contradictions between religions are obvious to the logic of a five-year old. If asked how many

---

[3] It's ironic that Gautama's followers chose to worship him. What's with these humans who seem to long for something to worship?

clickers[4] are in the living room, he will know the answer immediately: one, more than one, or none. Either there are many gods, one god, or no gods. No culture in the world will hold to any two of these beliefs *at the same time*. An individual may choose to believe in many gods at some point, and later (maybe even on the same day!) change his belief to one god, but this 'either/or' logic hounds us constantly.

Buddhists, Sikhs and Hindus should "tolerate" and respect each other's freedom to hold their own religious conviction, but they do not, even for a moment, believe that each other's views of god(s) to be *true* in any real sense of the word. Even though Hinduism and Buddhism are very similar, Buddhism came out of Hinduism because Gautama disagreed with Hinduism!

Therefore, when our "enlightened" Western pluralists claim that these faiths are really one and the same, their arrogance replaces their logic with . . . well, illogical arrogance. Sikhism claims that polytheism dishonors and disgraces the one true God. Sikhs shake their heads in disgust when people in the West claim that their monotheism is

---

[4] A "clicker" is an instrument of power used to control which television show the family is watching. The desire to control the universe arises early in a child and therefore the child will have no trouble answering this question.

just another form of polytheism.

The same comparison holds true for modern Judaism, Christianity, and Islam. Each one of these believes in monotheism. No adherent of these three religions would agree, however, that this one item is the only thing that matters about these three religions. On the contrary! All three claim that their one God is quite different from the other two!

Islam believes that Jesus was a prophet, but rejects the idea that Jesus died on a cross, or that He rose from the dead. The Koran describes these beliefs as blasphemous.[5] Modern Judaism rejects Jesus as their Messiah, claiming that Jesus was just one of many false messiahs.[6] Central to the biblical faith is the conviction that Jesus is equal with God, that He took on human form as a Jew during the Roman occupation of Palestine, that He is the Son of God, that He purposely and intentionally died on a cross for mankind's sins, and that He rose from the dead to prove that He was sinless and right about everything else. The resurrection of Jesus Christ is non-negotiable, but the central core of the biblical faith. The logical 'either/or' paradigm kicks in. Either Jesus is God or He isn't. He is the Messiah or He isn't. It doesn't work to say, "in my eyes He is,

---

[5] Suras 4.157; 5.75-78.
[6] Talmud: b. Sanhedrin 43a.

but in your eyes He isn't." What a person believes doesn't change the *fact* of who Jesus is, one way or the other.

Years ago in Austria, in a college class on philosophy, one of the students made the statement, "I deny the existence of God." Our professor, who was a staunch atheist, engaged the student by presenting him with two options.

"There is a tree in the room." The professor pointed toward an empty part of the room and asked everyone to imagine a real tree standing there. "If I say, 'I deny the existence of a tree in the room,' what does that mean?" He waited a few seconds, and then continued, "The tree is either there or not. So what do I mean when I say, 'I deny the existence of a tree in the room'? The tree is there, whether I choose to believe in its existence or not."

He continued with his second option. "However, there is no tree in the room. What do I mean, then, when I say, 'I deny the existence of a tree in the room'? Why am I denying the existence of something that doesn't exist?" He then turned to the student and asked, "What do you mean when you say, 'I deny the existence of God'?"

The student yelled at him, "Yes, I believe that God exists, but I hate Him!" The professor chose to change the subject at that point. Obviously, the student's denial of God did not originate through logical, thoughtful deduction, but from some bad experiences which he chose to blame on God.

When I spoke with the professor afterwards, I asked him about his staunch atheism. He answered honestly, "I choose to not believe in God, and if He does exist, then I will discover that I'm wrong."

Being that he was a well-read, highly intelligent person, I pointed out that some other famous philosophers chose to believe in the existence of God. Since all philosophers have the same evidence available to them, I asked him why he chose disbelief, instead of belief in God.

He needed no time to formulate his answer. "I don't want a God who rules over me. I don't believe that humans should have to submit to a higher power."

The fact that he might be wrong did not disturb him. He chose his belief based on what he wanted, not on what might be true or false.

Do all religions lead to God? No. The differences between religions cannot be brushed off the table with a simple, "All religions are the same because God loves everybody." The adherents of most religions believe that God only loves the followers of their religion.

Our second question: How do we get along with each other?

CHAPTER THREE

## TOLERANCE

In 1993 the United Nations declared that 1995
should become the "International Year for
Tolerance." That year was marked by thousands of
cultural events and conferences promoting
tolerance. Following that year, a violent war broke
out in Yugoslavia that divided that country into five
countries. That war was fueled by religious tensions
that had been suppressed for over fifty years. On
Sept. 11th Muslim terrorists apparently did not
recognize the U.N.'s year of tolerance. The U.N.'s
decision was merely wishful thinking with no
enforcement capabilities.

Some people confuse tolerance with pluralism.

"You Christians are really arrogant to claim that your religion is the only right religion."

Approximately two billion people believe that Christianity—Roman Catholicism and Protestantism combined—reigns supreme. One-third of the world thinks that the other two-thirds is wrong. One billion people believe in Islam. Islamists believe that Allah is the only god in existence. Nineteen percent of the world's population believes that eighty-one percent of the world has been misguided. Atheism claims that all religions are wrong. Since most atheists exist in Europe and North America, atheists are a very small minority of the world's other adherents to all the other religions. Therefore, a very small percentage (two percent?) of humanity (atheists) believes that the vast majority (ninety-eight percent?) of humanity (all non-atheists) are wrong.

As noted previously, pluralism receives the prize for having discovered religious vegetable soup. Pluralism has discovered (or rather, assumed, since pluralism is an ideology, not a scientific study) that all religions are wrong for believing that all other religions are wrong. Brilliant. While thoroughly disregarding a massive amount of anthropology research across seven continents, pluralism claims to have discovered something that *all* faiths have failed to perceive, i.e., that there are really no serious differences between religions after all. Adherents of pluralism seem to have one of two problems. Either they believe that they are smarter than everyone else (which is an insult to non-pluralists), or they are simply blind to their own intellectual dishonesty (which removes them from any serious discussion of the differences between religions).

Tolerance is *not* a willingness to accept another person's viewpoint as *valid or right*. This definition would require a Muslim to accept Jesus as the only Savior of the world, or an atheistic Buddhist to accept all three million Hindu gods as valid.

Neither can we honestly equate tolerance with pluralism. Tolerance, by definition, consists of at least two opinions that do not agree with one another. From the Latin, tolerance means *to endure* opposition.

My parents did not like my contemporary music, but they endured (put up with), i.e., tolerated it. They didn't agree with it; they didn't accept it; they didn't like it, but they let me listen to it, i.e., they tolerated it. My parents were not pluralists. They didn't agree with every kind of music. They tolerated it.

Great Britain did not agree with Hitler when he invaded Poland before the start of WWII, but they endured/allowed him to do it, i.e., they tolerated it. When Hitler finally attacked France, they refused to tolerate that action, and they declared war on Germany. The government of Great Britain was not pluralistic. They did not agree with Hitler; they tolerated him, to a point; then they stopped being tolerant.

Because the United States promotes the separation of church and state, America is tolerant of all religions. This tolerance does not extend to a religion that advocates and attempts to practice the destruction of another religion. Many religions may believe that they are the only true religion, but in America, these exclusive religions are forced to be tolerant and to allow other religions to co-exist along side of them. Adherents of Christianity may believe that Jesus is the only Savior of the world, but Christianity is tolerant when it allows people to freely worship in an Islamic Mosque or Buddhist temple down the block.

Strongly held beliefs, however, are not, in and of themselves, presumptuous or bigoted. A person who holds strong beliefs may be tolerant or intolerant regardless of their beliefs. Religions are not tolerant or intolerant. People are. A person is not intolerant because he believes that he holds the only right religion. A person becomes intolerant when he no longer allows other religions to co-exist alongside his religion.

If we insist that everyone agree that every religion is *right*, that is intellectually ridiculous and culturally insensitive. It says to people of other cultures and other religions that they are really only a small subset of a pluralistic idea of religion, and they should stop promoting their own distinctive features. This forced pluralism removes any healthy dialogue between people of different faiths. This lack of discussion and debate negates the individual's right to choose his own religion, which differs from other religions. It goes back to the tree in the room. Religions are different from one another, and simply claiming they are not, does not make their differences evaporate.

True tolerance is both intellectually stimulating and culturally sensitive. Serious discussion between different religions forces a person to inspect his or her own religion more closely. Respecting other cultures, without agreeing with them, promotes world unity. We can be free to contradict but not disrespect others, to persuade but not force others. We really, really, really need *true* tolerance in our world today.

# Intellectual Laziness

Pluralism is a sham for those who don't want to intellectually challenge their own presuppositions and beliefs. When our beliefs are challenged, we take the easier way out and accuse those who disagree with us of being intolerant. It is easier to assume that all religions are fundamentally the same, than it is to study a couple of religions to discover a few basic differences.

I taught a college class on *Comparative Religions* for three years. At the beginning of the semester, a gentleman had wanted to audit the class, which I agreed to. After the first class, he dropped out, because he said that he believed that all religions were right. He didn't want to be told that any of them were right or wrong; he just wanted to learn about them.

A couple of days after that person dropped the class, the students had to take a scheduled weekly quiz. One of the questions on the quiz was as follows. Try to answer the question before you continue reading.

Question #5:

Buddhism = there are no gods.
Hinduism = there are millions of gods.
Islam = there is one god.

Answer (check the correct box):

___ Buddhism is right.
___ Hinduism is right.
___ Islam is right.
___ All three religions are right.

The quiz took five minutes, and we graded it in class. No one checked the fourth box. A heavy discussion broke out about the fact that I had not included Christianity as an option. Most in the class felt that I had slanted the quiz away from Christianity. Some of the students had checked the third box (Islam is right), but they did not believe that Islam had the right god.

I told them that I had included this question to discover if the students understood, intuitively, the 'either/or' principle of logic. If a student checked any of the first three boxes, they would have passed that question. If a student checked the fourth box, they would have missed that question. Groans and boos followed, but they got the point. Even if they did not agree with the first three answers, the fourth answer could not be right. No student had checked the fourth box.

Acquiring information about religions, but refusing to compare them in order to discover how they disagree with one another, exhibits intellectual laziness. If we discover some discrepancies in our own religion, we might be forced to admit that we could be wrong about God and our relationship with Him (or lack of a relationship with Him).

So, when we are faced with something that seems to contradict our own personal beliefs, we have a choice. We can ignore it and assume that the contradiction doesn't exist, as in the movie, *The Matrix*: "There is no spoon."[7] This allows us to avoid thinking too hard about things that might force us to change our lifestyles.

Whichever path we choose, either hiding behind religious intolerance or not thinking at all, pluralism actually leaves us with no faith at all. God remains a mystery. We are like the Athenians in the first century with altars to an unknown god.[8]

---

[7] The fantasy movie *The Matrix* postulated a parallel world in which one could simply deny the existence of something, and that something would not exist.

[8] The philosophers in Athens in Acts 17 had demanded that Paul explain his teaching about Jesus being raised from the dead. He began his speech by pointing to a statue that had been dedicated to "an unknown God" and then brought the conversation around to Jesus.

## Time to Accept Assumptions

### (We knew they were there all along)

Blaise Pascal, the famous French mathematician, once wrote in his booklet *Pensees*: "There is a God shaped vacuum in the heart of every man which cannot be filled by any created thing, but only by God, the Creator, made known through Jesus." People feel a sense of emptiness and loss without really knowing what's missing. If a higher power does exist, then it makes sense to expect some recognizable sign(s) in the world, at our human level, that can direct us in the right direction. It seems logical that a Creator God would not leave humans with nothing more than a bewildering pile of religions to confuse us. Instead of making the search difficult, like a complicated treasure hunt, someone looking for God would assume that God wants humans to find Him. And if He did leave us some information as to His existence, how can we *verify* the truthfulness of this information?

Before looking for this information, we need to make an *assumption* and then ask ourselves one *question*. **The assumption**: there is a Higher Being. This book will make no attempt to prove the existence of God. A person cannot honestly claim to be seeking God or wanting to get to know Him at any level, if that person does not believe that God exists. That person may not be certain that God exists, but an open, searching mind will overcome this uncertainty. Nothing can overcome a prior disbelief in God's existence. A person has to be open to the possibility of God's existence before a serious search can begin.

For example, imagine telling your marriage partner that you don't believe that she exists. It goes without saying that she will not be pleased. This attitude works with God in the same way. If a person does not believe that God "is," then there is no basis for even continuing the conversation, and pleasing Him won't happen, either. Since God created humanity, and not the other way around, God adds one more criteria for pleasing Him and getting to know Him. Anyone who seeks Him has to also believe that God rewards those who seek Him.[9] They have to believe that God is not arbitrarily rejecting some people who want to find Him, just because He had a bad day or doesn't like their hairstyle. They have to believe that God is good and will keep His promise: if you seek God, you will find God.

As noted earlier under the topic of Pluralism,

---

[9] This is foundational to understanding man's search for God. Hebrews 11:6, "And without faith it is impossible to please Him, for he who comes to God must believe that He is, and that He is a rewarder of those who seek Him."

the answer to the question, "Does God exist?" is always a resounding "yes!" in the mainstream of every culture in the world, even among the Buddhists today. Only a few "brilliant" professors, perceiving themselves to be mentally superior to the majority of mankind, postulate the non-existence of higher beings that could directly influence the material world of the 21$^{st}$ century. Other people simply avoid the topic of God, running from the questions, hoping that, if there is a God, closing their eyes in denial will make him disappear. If the reader believes that the spoon might be there (remember *The Matrix*?), keep reading. If the reader does not like the existence of spoons, then the journey ends before it starts. Ignore the question, "Does God exist?" and give this book to someone else to read.

**The question**: If the reader wants to find God, where should he or she start?

CHAPTER FOUR

---

**VERIFY, VERIFY, VERIFY!**

Believing that God exists and that He wants people to find Him does not relieve us from being somewhat skeptical. Skepticism protects us from being deceived by false gods. We need to question the sources of information about God for their authenticity and accuracy. At the same time, we need to be careful that we do not reject some "content" about God because it disagrees with what we want to believe about Him.

Sometimes, for reasons unknown, even with overwhelming authentic and accurate evidence, we may *choose* to reject the evidence as insufficient, or we may *choose* to ignore it simply because we do not want to believe the evidence. *Our will* makes that choice, apart from any evidence from any source. This means that my choice will only affect what I believe, not the facts (reality) or truth. I may choose to *believe* something that is *not* a fact nor true, and I may choose to *deny* a fact or a truth, which *is*, in reality, a fact and a truth. Therefore, facts and truth exist apart from any one person's beliefs.

This demonstrates the priority of the human will over the provision of evidence. If a person is seeking the facts and truly wants to find them, then that person's will dictates the choice of how to handle the evidence. If a person is not seeking the facts and wants to believe some other viewpoint, then it is very unlikely that any amount of evidence will cause that person to believe the truth of the evidence presented. A person has to be *open* (his personal volition/will) to all the evidence available by the end of the seeking process, or that person's conclusions will conform to his previous presuppositions that forbid the acceptance of the evidence. We humans want what we want, often in spite of the kind or amount of information received.

On the other hand, skepticism at the beginning of the process of seeking the facts and truth is a good thing. A true skeptic will continue his quest and will eventually arrive at the truth, because he will not cease to search for and discover all the evidence available. Once he believes that he has enough valid evidence, he will choose to believe the evidence, while continually questioning the initial assumptions against any further evidence.

## Verify!

Which sources tell us about God, and how do we determine if the evidence in these sources is valid? Where do we start looking? Since humans have not been able to jump up into heaven and have a heart-to-heart talk with God, we have to wait until He chooses to start the process of revealing Himself to humanity. We can't climb up to a higher level of existence. If there is going to be any communication between different levels of existence, then the Higher level has to initiate the process. For example, animals don't study humans in laboratories. Normally, animals don't attempt to communicate with humans. An animal can't become a human. Usually, animals want to stay away from humans. In the same way, if God wants to communicate with us, He will need to reach out to us in a tangible way that we can't miss: something that screams at us that He exists and at a level we can understand.

We have a boatload of sources claiming to be from

God. How can we *verify* the myriad of spiritual claims accosting us from every religion on the planet? Most of the world's religions are *unverifiable*. They must be taken on faith alone. This does not mean they are not true, just that we can't prove whether they are true or not. Buddhism, for instance, sprang from one man's experience under a tree. Siddhartha Gautama was a sixth century B.C. Indian prince. He rejected his posh lifestyle and spent seven years seeking something more. At the end of those seven years, while sitting alone under a tree one night, "enlightenment" dawned (Buddha means "enlightened one"). This enlightenment consisted of his view of the true goal of life (the negation of self and desire), the nature of life after death (*karma* and rebirth) and numerous ethical and food disciplines required of those wishing to reach Nirvana, which is the ultimate achievement of non-existence.

None of this information could be *verified*. Buddha's followers simply had to believe that Buddha was telling the truth. Buddha offered no evidence of his experience under the tree—just his word, alone. Perhaps it was all true, but we can't verify that because there is no way to test it.

Islam is similar to Buddhism in its lack of *verifiability*. Muhammed was a seventh century A.D. rich Arabian caravan owner. He claimed to have received his revelations privately through the mystical appearance of the angel, Gabriel. Muhammed said that Gabriel gave him ethical and social rules, many closely resembling Jewish and Christian teachings, while others directly contradicted these viewpoints. There were no witnesses who saw or heard Gabriel speaking to Muhammed. And Muhammed offered no evidence of his experiences with Gabriel—just his word, alone. Perhaps it may all be true, but we can't verify that because there is no way to test it.

These two examples highlight our problem of finding God. These religions require *blind* faith, that is, faith based on no *verifiable* evidence. If Christianity can offer no better verifiable evidence than these two examples, then any religion will suffice to make us feel better without really knowing if we are in line with reality or not.

So, we need to ask ourselves, are there any spiritual traditions that provide any *verifiable* claims? Has God, Himself, left us with any signs that we can analyze in order to determine if the unknown God that the apostle Paul referred to[10], actually exists? And if He does exist, can we know more about Him than just what the existence of the universe teaches us?

---

[10] Acts 17:23.

Wouldn't it be nice if God simply chose to circumvent the religious smorgasbord and gave each human a personal revelation of Himself? And in order to be fair, wouldn't it be nice if every person had an equal chance to find God, and God would give each person the same opportunity to discover His existence?

The apostle Paul, in the book of Romans[11] in the Bible (which can be verified![12]), starts with this premise and points out the most obvious and logical signpost pointing to a higher being: the universe. Paul argues that the universe reveals to us the most basic and observable aspects of what God is like in two areas. Paul says that the universe's existence demonstrates (1) that God is far more powerful than we are, and (2) that God is inherently different than we are.

God demonstrates His power through the fact that He created the universe. Humans didn't put it there, and only a handful of evolutionists in the Western world accept the idea that the universe just happened. Every culture in the world interacts with the universe and ascribes its existence to some sort of deity or deities.

---

[11] Romans 1:18-21.

[12] F. F. Bruce, *New Testament Documents: Are They Reliable?* Leicester: IVP Press, 1981, 6th ed.

God demonstrates His differentness by creating a universe out of nothing. We humans can take raw materials and build things, but we can't take nothing and create raw materials. This places God in a category all by Himself. God is not like humans; He is intrinsically different.

This knowledge about God usually produces fear in people. If God can do all that, then He can destroy humans just as easily. Most religions have developed a system whereby they attempt to keep God away from them, because they live in fear of what He might do to them, if they do something that makes Him mad. They're not sure what will make Him mad, but every culture has a concept of right and wrong. Different cultures have different rights and wrongs, but every culture supports a set of ethics and morals.

Again in the book of Romans 1:18-21, the apostle Paul wrote that God put this sense of morality inside of every human being. A few humans may choose to deny this basic sense of right and wrong, but if someone attacks them, they will claim that it is wrong to be attacked.[13] If Paul is correct in his

---

[13] One of my student editors told me that this sentence sounds very much like a line out of C. S. Lewis' book, *Mere Christianity*. Since I read that book years ago, I don't remember any specifics in that book. Therefore I will give credit to C. S. Lewis for the influence he has had on my life.

assertions, this sense of morality, combined with the knowledge that God is eternally more powerful and completely different from humans, gives us a broad, picture of the basic nature of God. God is powerful enough to create a universe. He is a Higher Being, whom we can't reach without Him coming down to our level. And He is interested in right and wrong.

Where do we go from here?

The *fact* of the stars and the universe tells the serious seeker that God is very powerful, since He created those stars. These material objects, however, tell us nothing of God's character. Is God good or evil? Is He personal or just some accidental force? If He is personal, does He want to take care of us when we have problems? Does He have any rules that we're supposed to follow, so He doesn't get mad at us?

We can't answer these questions without more specific information. And we can't get this information, unless God gives it to us.

*Yet God has done just that.* Imagine the implications. God would have to be personal in order to communicate at that level. An impersonal force might accidently pop out some stars into the vastness of space, but an inanimate force can never produce animate life, and we are still left with the unanswered question of the origin of the material universe. Imagine a personal God who *can* and *wants to communicate personally* with *you*! Think of the people you would love to get to know better. Then place them in a priority list. Now imagine discovering that the person at the top of your list wants to get to know *you*. Visualize a two-way relationship in which you and God are talking about each other. You get to tell God about your dreams, your fears, your plans, your loves, and God listens to everything. Then you ask God his view of everything you've told Him. He assures you that He wants your best, and that, because He is God, He will guarantee that you will receive what is best for you personally. He has only one request: Trust Him.

Why would God *want* to give you what is best for you? Is this some temporary hobby that God has, or does this guarantee arise from something deeper in the nature of God? A story might provide us with the answer.

A four-story apartment house caught on fire,[14] and just as the entire building was engulfed in flames, a little girl's voice was heard coughing for help. She was trapped on the third floor in the only room still intact. A firemen went back into the flames, up three flights of crumbling stairs, kicked in the door, grabbed a chair, threw it through the window,

---

[14] The author received this story from a fireman.

pulled the young girl out from under the bed, and without looking, leaped out the window, just as the room exploded into flames. He wrapped himself around the little girl and turned his body around so that he would land on his back when he hit the ground, so the girl would be protected as much as possible from the fall. His buddies saved his life by getting the safety net in place at the last second. When the reporters asked his friends why he would do something like that, they replied, "Because that's who he is."

Likewise, that's why God *wants* to communicate with you and why His guarantee is certain: Because that's who He is. As we search deeper into God's nature, we will discover God can't help Himself. He *loves* revealing what He is like to us, and out of His character, giving us what is best for us.

CHAPTER FIVE

---

**EXPERIENCE, TRADITION and REASON**

So *how* does God communicate with us? Scholars have generally studied four sources for this knowledge: Experience, Tradition, Reason and the Bible itself.

<u>Experience</u>

One of my friends once told me, "I rotate churches and religious services every week." He pointed toward his bookshelf, which prominently displayed a variety of religious books.

"Why?" I asked.

"I believe that God exists in all religions," he answered, "and I want to experience Him everywhere."

"How do you know when you've experienced Him?"

"Well, a person can't know that. I just want to feel close to him each time I go to a religious center."

The German atheist Ludwig Feuerbach critiqued religion as nothing more than human self-awareness. He stated that God could not be proven through experience, and therefore religion was just a technical term for categorizing one's personal experience. The majority of the world, however, believes that the supernatural can be experienced by humans in some way. The obvious weakness of attempting to learn about God through experience is a complete lack of certainty. Each individual can claim that he has experienced God, but that brings us no further than Feuerbach's thesis. Our god-experience could have been a dream or a nightmare, or the feeling we get when we meditate on a brilliant sunset or a cascading waterfall. Even if God can be experienced, a higher level of certainty would be desirable. Experience requires no information about God; it just requires human emotions.

However, doesn't every human have an inner sense of God? Maybe they do, but again, that is not verifiable. It may be like the story of the tree falling in the forest, but nobody hears the sound. The sound is there (factual, verifiable physics), but no one witnessed it (experience). Therefore, every human could possibly have a built-in sense of a higher being, but the only way to know for sure would be for God to tell us that.

The other side of the coin is equally unverifiable. Volker was a student in Austria who claimed that there was no higher being. I asked him if he had had all the experiences in the entire universe. He said no. I then asked him if it could be possible that God existed outside of his own personal experiences. He responded, "How did you learn to argue so well?" His lack of seriousness in seeking God ended our discussion.

The Bible actually says (Psalm 14:1 for the Jews and Psalm 53:1 for the non-Jews) that a person who claims there is no God is a fool. The reason for this description goes back to the will of the person. Since a person cannot claim to "know" that there is no God, but does make such a claim, the motivation for this claim cannot be a thorough evaluation of the evidence, since the evidence is too vast to research in order to arrive at a conclusive claim that God does not exist. Again, the Bible states that this person does know that God exists, but actively rejects this truth by internally suppressing it. "For the wrath of God is revealed from heaven against all ungodliness and unrighteousness of men *who suppress the truth* in unrighteousness" (Romans 1:18). "Professing to be wise, they became fools" (Romans 1:22).

## Traditions, Creeds and Liturgies

After Jesus rose from the dead and all the apostles had passed away, people in the churches began to develop different ways of thinking about God. Many traditions sprang up that contained ideas about God. Jesus had previously condemned the traditions of the Pharisees because traditions directly contradicted God's commandments: "Why do you also transgress the commandments of God because of your traditions?" (Matt. 15:3-9) Jesus pointed out that such traditions led people to worship God in vain (useless and detrimental worship!) because these traditions taught human ideas as if God had decreed these ideas.

In order to avoid this sin, the early believers took their traditions, creeds and liturgies straight out of the Bible. The Apostle Paul praised the believers in Corinth for following some traditions. "Now I praise you, brethren, that you remember me in all things and keep the traditions just as I delivered them to you" (1 Cor. 11:2). One of the earliest creeds came out of 1 Timothy 3:16:

> And without controversy great is the
>     mystery of godliness:
> [God] was manifested in flesh,
> Justified in Spirit,
> Seen by angels,
> Preached among the Gentiles,
> Believed on in the world,
> Received up in glory.

Some believe that Philippians 2:5-11 was one of the earliest hymns that God gave Paul as inspired text. It's too bad that God did not give Paul the music to accompany the lyrics. That would have made it much easier to memorize for those in later centuries.

These early traditions, creeds and liturgies were used to bring a systematized order to the teaching and practices of the early Christians and their churches. Later on, the Nicene Creed (among others) attempted to formulate a simple statement of the Christian faith as a guard against heresy in the Church.

Nicene Creed:

We believe in one God the Father Almighty, Maker of heaven and earth, and of all things visible and invisible.

And in one Lord Jesus Christ, the only-begotten Son of God, begotten of the Father before all worlds, God of God, Light of Light, Very God of Very God, begotten, not made, being of one substance with the Father by whom all things were made; who for us men, and for our salvation, came down from heaven, and was incarnate by the Holy Spirit of the Virgin Mary, and was made man, and was crucified also for us under Pontius Pilate. He suffered and was buried, and the third day he rose again according to the Scriptures, and ascended into heaven, and sits on the right hand of the Father. And he shall come again with glory to judge both the quick and the dead, whose kingdom shall have no end.

And we believe in the Holy Spirit, the Lord and Giver of Life, who proceeds from the Father and the Son, who with the Father and the Son together is worshipped and glorified, who spoke by the prophets. And we believe in one holy catholic and apostolic Church. We acknowledge one baptism for the remission of sins. And we look for the resurrection of the dead, and the life of the world to come. Amen.[15]

---

[15] (http://www.creeds.net/ancient/nicene.htm)

As the years passed, many traditions, creeds and liturgies sprang up that had not originated from the clear statements of Scripture, but they came from nothing more than theological speculation. Tevye, the father in the movie "Fiddler on the Roof," portrays a religious Jewish man who has no idea why his religious traditions came into existence. These types of traditions eventually dictated the teaching and lifestyle of the followers of a particular group of the Jewish and Christian religions. The lack of any clear support from the Bible allowed these traditions and creeds to be used by those in power to keep themselves in power. And because these traditions, creeds and liturgies were not checked against Scripture, many of the traditions and liturgies received equal status with the Bible (as "inspired" by God). Forms of worship (traditions) and liturgies became enshrined in a community, and if anyone deviated from them, those people were kicked out of the religious services. However, when a person moved to another religious community, the traditions and liturgies were different, and there was no continuity between the groups.

This raised the unanswerable question: How can we know for sure that the traditions, the creeds and the liturgies actually teach us the truth about God? Since humans made up these traditions, creeds and liturgies, what do they have to do with God's character?

Vincent of Lérins (died c. 445) attempted to clarify the situation when he made the statement that the way we know we are right about the things pertaining to God is to "hold that faith which has been believed everywhere, always, by all." He was referring to the traditions and liturgy that had developed up to his time. The difficulty with this view, however, was that more and more traditions emerged, and contradicting traditions caused more fights than unity. Things did not improve as the Roman Catholic Church grew in the Middle Ages. After the Protestant Reformation, little consistency between traditions existed among the many diverse religious groups that engulfed Europe. The many traditions presented no standard of truth by which to evaluate their contradicting claims. Traditions, creed, and liturgies remain bogged down in conflicting claims about the right way of thinking about God.

## Reason

Right now you are using reason to understand this sentence. We apply literal hermeneutics,[16] which

---

[16] Henry A. Virkler and Karelynne Ayayo. *Hermeneutics: Principles and Processes of Biblical Interpretation.* Grand Rapids: Baker Book House, 1981, 2007.

includes normal rules of grammar and basic logic to continue on to reading the next sentence. Even though we may not completely comprehend an issue, we do not accept obvious contradictions. We might misunderstand or misinterpret information, but when new information surfaces, or we discover inconsistencies in our previous viewpoint, we re-evaluate and form updated conclusions. We subconsciously apply our reason to every aspect of our lives. We use our reason in an attempt to explain the sciences, our dreams, our emotions, and our relationships. I say "attempt," because we realize that we can never be one hundred percent correct (except in the area of simple mathematics, where two plus two will always equal four). Every science continually changes as additional information is discovered. Assuming that we want truth, our reason is limited only by incomplete information (and our will, as indicated in a previous chapter). Some theologians believe that human reason has been damaged, or even rendered completely corrupt, due to man's rebellion against God. To whatever degree our minds can process correctly, our reason is dependent on the amount and the validity of the information received and evaluated.

---

Some theologians believe that we need to understand God by studying man, since God created man. The problem with this approach, however, is that we don't really know how much man is like God. The only way to learn that, is for God to tell us, and that means that our understanding of God has to begin with God speaking first. In any case, if we study ourselves, we are the object of our own investigation. That approach doesn't allow complete objectivity. We can end up deceiving ourselves by relying on subjective and unclear information and conclusions. This will then cloud our vision when we attempt to study God through humanity. We will have to discover how to study God first, in order to understand ourselves.

When we apply our reason to information from the universe about the Creator, we are faced with two limitations. As mentioned above, our reasoning powers are not infinite or perfect. Second, the universe does not use words. Creation is God's body language. Scholars call this language "General Revelation." It is "general" because everybody can experience it. Everyone can witness the vastness, the variety, and the order throughout the universe. No one can escape this information.

Combining philosophy, logic, and this available-to-all body language has produced various theories that attempt to "prove" God's existence. God never attempts to prove His own existence. I will, therefore, simply describe these theories as a step toward understanding how philosophy and logic have been used to give us potential insights into God's existence.[17]

## The Cosmological Argument

Simply put, the Cosmological Argument states that because everything has a cause, something without a cause had to cause everything else. Few people believe that the universe came into existence out of nothing without something creating it. That something is God. The uncaused Creator caused everything else to come into existence.

One of my previous co-workers had spent twenty-five years in Africa as a missionary and had learned carpentry during that time. After returning to the States, he continued woodworking as a hobby. When you walked into his house, every single piece of wooden furniture had come into existence from this carpenter's hand of over thirty years of experience. Every time someone came into his living room for the first time, they saw a large,

---

[17] There's a caveat. This line of reasoning can only take us so far before we hit two walls: the limitations of this information for learning about God and, as mentioned above, our desire or lack of desire to allow this information about God to motivate us to seek further information, which God makes available to us another way.

ornate grandfather clock standing against the far wall. They would exclaim, "Who made that? It's beautiful!" My co-worker never answered, "Oh, it just simply appeared out of nowhere one morning." No, that clock had a creator.[18]

I once attended a high school science fair in Vienna, Austria. One of the most popular exhibits at that conference was a perpetual motion machine put together by two brilliant students from the Japanese International School. Those two young boys received one of the highest awards. Before the awards were given out, there was plenty of time to talk with the students about their projects. One of the boys made the statement that their project demonstrated that there was no need to believe in a higher power, because the machine ran on its own and produced its own energy. One of the other students asked, "So who made the machine in the first place?"

Children will often ask the question, "Mommy, who made God?" We can help them understand God as the Creator by teaching them the difference between God's creative acts of bringing matter out of nothing, versus humanity's ability to take created matter to "make" things. God "creates" things out

---

[18] If a human with limited abilities can produce such a work of art after 30 years of experience, what can God produce with His power and abilities?

of nothing, while we, humans, "make" things out of what God has created.

## The Teleological Argument

The Teleological Argument is a subcategory of the cosmological one. Since there is evidence of harmony, order, and design *within* the cosmos, this demonstrates that the universe has a purpose ("tele" means = "purpose"). Why is there so much order, if it was not designed for a purpose? We have endless examples in human experience, which are used to support this argument. Why do people build hospitals? Cities? Can we think of anything humans have built that had no purpose? Even art, which can be interpreted in numerous ways, has the purpose of enjoyment. Numerous mathematicians have claimed that there has to be a Creator, because a simple "poof" from nothing cannot account for how much order exists in the mathematical world. The preciseness of mathematics could not have developed by random chance.

## The Ontological Argument

The Ontological ('ont' means "being") Argument promotes two ideas of "greater." It's greater to exist than to not exist, therefore, God exists. And God has to be greater than anything else, or He would be equal to something in creation, negating His ability to create everything. Thus God is the greatest thing that can be humanly imagined. This "greatest" thing cannot be an inanimate (dead) object, because a living, eternal, personal God would be greater. Therefore, this argument concludes that God exists and is greater than anything within creation, which includes the imagination of man. This viewpoint has similarities to the Cosmological logic in that the greatest Being will have to be the Cause of all else (the Creator).

## The Moral Argument

The Moral Argument teaches that all humans (even atheists) have an inbred sense of right and wrong. Everyone wants "justice" in their lives. This sense of right and wrong has been labeled as a conscience. The conscience is like a box. Every human has this box, but the contents of the box varies from culture to culture, person to person. There is some sense of right and wrong in every box, because every culture puts its own standards of right and wrong in the box. God, however, gives every human being the box (conscience). Animals apparently do not have a conscience, nor varying content. They live on the survival of the fittest. Granted, sometimes people act like animals, but even the exceptions have their own value system of right and wrong. A murderer may claim that murder is okay, but he will violate his own code when he attempts to defend himself against someone else who wants to kill him.

Therefore, the framework (box), or our ideas that right and wrong exist, did not come from humanity or from the animal world. It had to come from a higher power: God (which might indicate that God is inherently good since He developed the box of right and wrong).

These "proofs" prove nothing, although collectively they make a good case for the existence of God, as long as we remember that God never attempts to prove His own existence. In fact, no religion begins with that Higher Power passing out a handbook on apologetics to prove his/her existence. These "proofs" demonstrate the ways we use our reason in our attempts to verify God's existence.

However, we want to know more about this God who exists. We want to know how He communicates with us. We've looked at the sources of experience, tradition, and reason in seeking an answer to this question, but we have discovered their lack of verification. We want more certainty of God's communication about Himself to us. Can our fourth source, the Bible, stand up to some level of verification?

# CHAPTER SIX

---

## THE BIBLE

The Bible is the most studied and verifiable book in existence. We don't need to resort to leaps of blind faith in order to justify our belief in the Bible's credibility and truthfulness. Some people come to the Bible with such an open mind, that they don't need any verification of its authenticity. They read it, accept it at face value, and discover that it changes them over time. Other people need some kind of verification, for fear of being deceived by another religious book. These people want enough verification to assure them that they are pursuing a worthy cause.

Verification checks a product, service, or system to see if it meets a set of design requirements, specifications, and regulations during the development and post-development stages of a project. Each field of study has its own set of validation criteria. A psychologist checks the emotional stability of his subjects throughout the session. Chemists do not use emotional stability to verify their chemicals. They check the amount of each substance before and after an experiment.

The verification of literature comes with its own set of criteria and procedures for determining its validity and trustworthiness. The criteria need to be *valid* for the product being verified (Am I building the right thing?), and the procedures need to be *carried out properly* to give each criteria good quality (Am I building it right?). Literature is validated by using "Retrospective Validation," which evaluates a text that has already come into existence.

The five criteria specific to literature validation, and specifically for the Bible, are consistency, coherence, comprehensiveness, reliability, and accuracy.

## Consistency

*Consistency* asks the negative question: Are there any *internal contradictions* within the text? If there are apparent contradictions, can they be explained by looking at the different contexts that might clarify the apparent contradictions? When people read the Bible and want to verify if it is consistent within itself, they often make the mistake of assuming that if they do not understand a text, then there must be a contradiction in the text. This is not true. Deeper study of the words in their context or the surrounding culture almost always clarifies an "apparent" contradiction.

## Coherence

*Coherence* asks the positive question: Does everything in the text *relate well* to the rest of the text, or is the text simply an assembly of disjointed statements? The sacred writings of many other main religions are nothing more than unconnected fragments of thoughts from beginning to end. This style of writing leaves out any flow of context by which the reader can judge the overall coherence of the entire book. The Bible is a history book with a running context from beginning to end, which allows the reader to see the connectedness of one statement in a given text with another statement in an entirely different text. Even in the book of Proverbs, the ideas connect with other parts of the Bible, thereby remaining congruent, even though the Proverbs appear to be random statements.

# Comprehensiveness

*Comprehensiveness* asks the question: Does the entire text cover all relevant experiences applicable to the topic of the texts? All of the personal experiences to have ever existed would require a book too large to contain them. Therefore, does the religious book contain enough experiences that cover enough aspects of life, so the reader can find some material for any given situation he is faced with in life? Whereas Buddhistic literature limits its life experiences to its founder, Gautama Siddharta, the Bible includes people from all walks of life and experiences between humans and God, humans and spirit beings (good and bad), humans and humans (good and bad) and humans and nature. The Bible addresses life's most controversial issues. It was written in three languages (Hebrew, Aramaic, and Greek) by at least forty authors over a period of fifteen-hundred years. *Comprehensiveness* will include precision in application to actual experiences, and scope that covers experiences of all kinds.

These three criteria relate to a piece of literature's worldview as a whole. The Bible is the only piece of literature that wears these three criteria like a well-fit shirt. The other religions' documents have no need for verification, because the followers of these religion require none. Their documents have never been able to stand up to these criteria anyway.

Along with the three C's[19] of verification, experts of literature also subject texts to two more specific criteria: reliability and accuracy.

## Reliability

*Reliability* asks the question: Did the authors actually write the documents as claimed, and can those authors be trusted to have stated the truth as they perceived it? In his book, *New Testament Documents: Are They Reliable?*, F. F. Bruce outlines the criteria for the evaluation of the Greek manuscripts in which the New Testament was originally written. Bruce demonstrates that the Bible is much more reliable that any other ancient document.

One interesting approach to the reliability of the Bible comes from D. James Kennedy and Jerry Newcombe entitled, *What if the Bible had never been Written?* Philip Schaff, the historian, wrote:

> Jesus of Nazareth, without money and arms, conquered more millions than Alexander, Caesar, Mohammed, and Napoleon; without science and learning, He shed more light on things human and divine than all philosophers

---

[19] Consistency, Coherence, and Comprehensiveness.

and scholars combined; without the eloquence of schools, He spoke such words of life as were never spoken before or since, and produced effects which lie beyond the reach of orator or poet; without writing a single line, He set more pens in motion, and furnished themes for more sermons, orations, discussions, learned volumes, works of art, and songs of praise than the whole army of great men of ancient and modern times.[20]

## Accuracy

*Accuracy* asks the question: Are the authors true to the actual facts of history, as opposed to having an agenda that skews the text from reality? For example, archaeology has often demonstrated the exactness of the Bible. Archaeology, of both the Old and New Testaments, continues to unearth names, dates, and locations that coincide with the statements found in the ancient biblical texts. The Biblical Archaeology Review[21] continues to solve such seeming dilemmas.

All five of these criteria can be summed up by the question, "Can we trust the Bible?" This author

---

[20] Schaff, *The Person of Christ*, p. 29.
[21] http://www.biblicalarchaeology.org/magazine/

need not treat this subject in much detail, since extensive work has already been carried out at all levels on this subject. Every Bible college, seminary, and doctoral program requires courses and seminars in "Apologetics," the title for this topic. Years ago, Josh McDowell wrote one of the most definitive books on this subject entitled, *Evidence That Demands a Verdict.* Translated into numerous languages, his book and many others like it, contains a detailed analysis of subjects that apply to the reliability and accuracy of the biblical text. Some of those topics include fulfilled prophecy, archaeological evidence, extra-biblical writings that collaborated the biblical text, scientific accuracy and foresight, the profound and extensive manuscript evidence, and the blatant honesty about the failings of many biblical heroes.

Before moving on to looking at the Bible directly as our primary source of specific information about God and His character, let's not undervalue the other three sources (experience, tradition, reason), even if they cannot provide the same verification as the Bible itself.

### Experience

*Experience.* God created us in His image, and therefore we are emotional and experiential beings. As we learn more about God's character, we will realize that He wants us to get emotionally involved with Him. He wants to awe us and give us elated emotions when we connect directly with Him in worship. He loves to hear our singing, even if it is off-key and horrendous, because He loves being praised, adored, and thanked for being Himself, as well as for what He had done for us and for others. God is like a grandfather[22] who loves playing with his grandchildren, pleasing them, holding them, and helping them to not hurt themselves (whether they are two years old or eighteen . . . eighteen year-olds make much bigger mistakes than two-year olds). He wants us to become ecstatic (a strong emotion!) about Him, about what He has done for us, and about what He is going to do for us.[23]

## Traditions

*Traditions.* God also desires order in our private world and in our churches.[24] Our traditions help

---

[22] God is not like a grandfather who closes his eyes to the sins of his grandchildren with the wave of a hand, saying, "They are just children. They can't help themselves." God never overlooks any sins, but desires repentance on the part of His children, so He can and will grant them forgiveness as often as they repent.

[23] He has given us access to Himself through Jesus. He wants to deepen our understanding and love for Him as He showers us with blessings unavailable to those who reject Him.

[24] First Corinthians 14:40, "Let all things be done decently and in order."

bring order to our lives. When they do not contradict the Scriptures, they can help us remember what God is like and what He desires of us. Although not God's Word like the Bible, our Christian music, whether hymns or contemporary songs, can teach us correct doctrine about God and about ourselves. Our order of service (traditions) can serve to help us focus our emotional (and experiential) response on God instead of having to figure out the new mechanics of a worship service that distracted us more than it should have. We do need change regularly,[25] but it needs to be understood that the change is intended to help us realize that God loves change, just as much as He loves consistency and order among His created humanity. He wants us to love what He loves, without losing our focus on Who He is, what He has done, what He is doing, and what He is going to do.

## Reason

*Reason.* God also created us with a mind that processes information. He wants us to use our minds to keep our *traditions* from becoming dead and lifeless, to keep our *emotions* from motivating us to make dumb decisions, and to *reason* through our study of the Bible to get to know Him better and

---

[25] We need to realize that God created the universe to change. Time, itself, is an instrument of change. The only things that do not change are God and His news about Jesus.

better. Eventually, we will come to realize that God never forced anybody to follow Him. He always addressed people primarily through the mind (and not emotions). He wants us to mentally analyze our traditions to discover where they succeed and where they fail to teach us about God and His character. Romans 12:2 reminds us of this truth, "And do not be conformed to this world, but be transformed by the renewing of your mind, that you may prove what is that good and acceptable and perfect will of God."

Therefore, without undervaluing our experiences or traditions, we will use our reason to study the Biblical text in order to discover what we can learn about God, His being, His activities, and His desires.

CHAPTER SEVEN

## THE ABILITY TO KNOW GOD

Can a person know what God is like? This question is easy and yet impossible to answer. It's easy because the answer is obvious. We "know" people. We know things about people, and we have different levels of relationships with them. We need knowledge about someone before we can have any kind of relationship with him or her. We know a little bit about the grocery store clerk, and our relationship is commensurate with our knowledge. We know more about grandma and even more about our best friend. Normally, a close relationship requires time to develop based on more and more knowledge gained in the process. Sometimes, we can develop a close relationship more quickly, but in either case, the knowledge of the other person has to be about that other person. If we do not receive any information about the other person, we can have no relationship with them. Therefore, when we speak of knowing God, we have to receive information about God. Volumes have been written about God, but if God does not exist, or if it is truly not possible to know anything at all about God, then all the religions in the world are ludicrous, man-made illusions, and all humans should be atheists. Theology (the study of God) would be nothing more than speculation and less interesting than a good science fiction novel.

Given that God does exist, some believe that God is incomprehensible, which they define as the inability to know anything about God. Some even use the Bible to prove that we can know nothing of God. Psalm 145:3 states that God's is unsearchable. Psalm 147:5 reveals that God's understanding is infinite or beyond measure. Romans 11:33 says that God judgments are unsearchable and His ways unfathomable. Taken in an absolute sense, as do some mystics, we can know nothing about God. If the absolute sense is our only option, then we should just give up and hope that God is a nice guy when we meet Him after we die.

As with any word, however, there is a range of

meaning, from one extreme to the next, depending on the context. I might say that physical equations are completely incomprehensible, but that is one extreme which uses an adverb (completely) to make my point. At the other extreme, I might say that my wife is incomprehensible, which is an exaggeration that means that men have difficulty understanding women. *It does not mean that we know nothing about them.*

If language were extremely incomprehensible, then language would be reduced to visual patterns. If God is completely incomprehensible, then He is limited in His ability to communicate Himself to humanity, which makes Him less than God, who is supposed to be able to do anything. If God is completely incomprehensible, then humanity is wasting its time talking about God, since no sense can be made of something that is completely incomprehensible. God is certainly beyond *all* comprehension, but the Bible also tells us that God *wants to communicate Himself* to us. Therefore, the definition of incomprehensible does not mean that we cannot understand *anything* about God. It means that we cannot understand *everything* about God. God's desire to make Himself known to us leads Him to make it possible for us to understand what He does choose to reveal to us.

If God can do anything within the limitations of His

character, then He is able to communicate those attributes of His character to us that we can understand. We will never be able to fully understand everything about God's character, but we can understand what He wants us to understand. His information about Himself will never be exhaustive about Himself, but what He tells us will still be true. In this sense we can know God by searching for and understanding the information He gives us about Himself. Based on that information, we can have a personal relationship with Him (in the same way we do with humans as discussed above).

Therefore, when we speak of knowing God, we recognize that this is about a growing relationship with God. We can never know exhaustively any one thing about another person or about God. This is not necessary to develop a close relationship with another person (human or God). As we study God's nature and character, we will grow to appreciate the fact that we can never know "too much" about God. We will simply continue to discover more and more about Him,[26] and this growing knowledge will grow our relationship with Him. We will never cease to learn new things about God. And every time we learn something new about God, these new "facts" about God will deepen our relationship with Him.

---

[26] Colossians 1:10, "increasing in the knowledge of God"

We will "know" God better at that point in time. Our motivation for this entire process can be grounded in the fact that God thinks about us far more than we think of Him. Psalm 139:17 reads, "How precious also are Your thoughts to me, O God! How vast is the sum of them!"

Does Heaven sound boring? If all we are going to do up there is sit around on a cloud and play a harp, that will get old in a hurry. We will enjoy having no sin to bother us there, but without any personal relationships to engage in, even heaven would be sterile and cold. Imagine the first time you met the love of your life. Imagine it even if it hasn't happened yet. Do you remember those intense silly feelings swamping your being and interrupting all other activities? As you got to know the person better, this infatuation wore off, and you began to appreciate the other person with a love that was more than just shallow emotions. I certainly love my wife more after forty years of marriage than I did when I gave her the engagement ring. This may be a very primitive example of our relationship with God when we arrive in heaven, but it raises some fun questions.

Have you ever been infatuated with God during your lifetime? Have you ever had a euphoric feeling that just takes over, and you find yourself singing praises to God automatically? I'm not sure if we want to label this as "infatuation" with God, but will people have these kinds of feelings constantly in heaven? During this lifetime, as we get to know God more, we trust Him more. And yet, eternity would have to run out before people will stop learning about God when they arrive in heaven. Will our infatuation mature into a deeper and deeper love throughout eternity?

The goal of this life is to get to know God better and better. Our life goal is not to seek emotional highs every Sunday morning. Our deeper, more mature emotions toward God depend on our knowledge of God, not the other way around. Chasing experiences only produces a shallow life, whereas a growing knowledge of God leads us deeper and deeper into His wisdom for working our way through everyday life situations, not just Sunday worship services.

Jesus is described in the Bible as claiming to be the personal representation of God in human form. He also claims to forgive sins, to be able to raise the dead, and to be the final Judge of all mankind at the end of time. All of these claims hinge on the first claim. If Jesus *is* the personal representation of God in human form, then anything Jesus claims will be true, regardless of mankind's acceptance or rejection of His person.

Jesus existed as a human before He was crucified,

and His followers got to know Him as a human. They never had a philosophical discussion about the possibility of having a personal relationship with Him. They had one. Their problem was recognizing, understanding and accepting His claims to be equal with God. That was a big stretch for strict monotheists who believed that anyone claiming to be equal with God should be stoned. Once they did accept His claims to be equal with God, they had no problem understanding how a person could have a personal relationship with God. They knew how to relate to human beings, and since Jesus was a human being and God, they could also have a relationship with God

This approach to providing humans with a personal relationship with God was also logical. God, the Higher Being, had to initiate the process. He had to come down to our human level so we could understand Him as a human, just as we understand other humans. Some people during the first and second centuries claimed that Jesus was just an illusion (Docetism), or that He had just been a spirit, but never human. This rejection of what the apostles wrote about Jesus negated any possibility of knowing God personally, as we know other people personally. Obviously, the Docetists never developed a personal relationship with God through Jesus as portrayed in the Bible.

At the beginning of this chapter I stated that if God does not exist, all humans should be atheists. If God does reveal Himself to everyone through His General Revelation, then why are there any atheists at all?

Let's answer this question with a question. Is it God's fault if people don't *choose* to recognize what He has revealed about Himself? Could it be possible that people have chosen to ignore what God has revealed to humanity? The answer is found in the Bible in the first chapter of the book of Romans in the New Testament. This chapter makes a number of statements about God, but the biggest item is God's response to those who ignore Him. He gets angry when people do not thank Him for having created them and having given them the universe to live in. Most people have trouble with an angry God, but since He created everything, then everything belongs to Him. If He desires to be thanked by what He made, He has every right to get angry when rejected.

The second question: If this information from God is available to everyone, why have many people misread it and developed so many religions, sects and cults in the world? Humans have a need for the divine in their lives, so they make up belief systems. Different cultures end up with different religions. Where did they get the need for the divine in their lives? If no God exists, why does the vast majority of humanity have a need for the divine in their lives? Atheists believe that religion exists to explain the unexplainable, until science advances enough to explain everything. Others believe that some guy started a rumor about God, and humans have never shaken themselves of that rumor. The Bible teaches that God created humans in God's image, that humans rebelled but still have a need for the divine in their lives, and that they don't want the True God, so they make up religions.

We have arrived at the front door. God exists. He created humans because He wants a personal relationship with each person. Humans sinned and rejected this relationship. God added humanity to His deity when Jesus was born, and then Jesus died on the Cross to offer us forgiveness for our sins. Jesus rose from the dead with an offer of a restored relationship with God, if we want it. And if we want it, God takes the next step and tells us all about Himself, or at least, what we can understand about Him at this point in our existence. The Bible, God's book, spells out God's attributes, i.e., God's character qualities. His attributes are intrinsic to His nature, His person. His attributes are a reflection of His character. We can't know everything about God, but we can know what He wants us to know about Him. And through our knowledge of His attributes, we can have a personal relationship with Him.

How do we study God's attributes? The best way is to develop a lifetime habit of reading His Bible from cover to cover, and always asking, "What does this passage tell me about God?" The second best way is to read some books on God's attributes. Many theology books contain chapters on the attributes of God, but these two books are the best place to start:

*Knowledge of the Holy*, A. W. Tozer
*Knowing God*, J. I. Packer

Seeking God? You *will* find Him.

# ANNOTATED BIBLIOGRAPHY

(in addition to the ones listed in the footnotes)

Dickson, John. *If I Were God, I'd Make Myself Clearer: Searching for Clarity in a World Full of Claims*. Sydney: Matthias Media, 2004. I picked this booklet up at an Alistar Begg's Pastor's Conference, and it sparked the idea for this booklet.

Schaeffer, Francis A. and J. P. Moreland. *Escape from Reason*. Downers Grove: IVP Books, 2006. I read this booklet three times during the summer of 1970. I met a friend that summer who took all ten weeks to explain it to me. I had always wondered if it couldn't have been put more simply. I hope this booklet does that.

Wolfe, David L. *Epistemology: The Justification of Belief*. Downers Grove: InterVarsity Press, 1982. Years ago I read this booklet and finally figured out why epistemology causes ulcers: to know how to know things. What about the things that we "just know"?

ABOUT THE AUTHOR

In addition to his prior church-planting and missionary work in Austria (15 years), Russia and the USA, Floyd Schneider has taught courses in Evangelism and Systematic Theology at Moody Bible Institute-Spokane in Washington State. Those courses motivated the writing of this booklet.

www.ingramcontent.com/pod-product-compliance
Lightning Source LLC
Chambersburg PA
CBHW060533030426
42337CB00021B/4242